Communication

Enhance Your Proficiency In Conversational Skills, Enhance Your Interpersonal Aptitude & Polish Your Public Speaking Abilities

(Effective Approaches For Cultivating A Contented Relationship; Sustaining A Well-Balanced And Satisfying Relationship)

Maria Wilkins

TABLE OF CONTENT

The Act Of Active Listening - A Fundamental Pillar Of Effective Communication...........................1

Create An Excellent Initial Impact 39

Avoiding Interruption 53

Fostering Empathy In A Professional Environment To Cultivate A Deeper Understanding Of Colleagues................................70

Communication In Relationships 99

Treasure Hunt.. 152

The Act Of Active Listening - A Fundamental Pillar Of Effective Communication

When individuals contemplate communication, their focus typically centers solely on oral expression. Nevertheless, as you are currently aware, proficient communication encompasses the element of providing feedback or a response, thus highlighting the significance of attentive listening.

The act of actively attending and comprehending auditory information holds immense significance in virtually every facet of your existence, as it grants you the ability to assimilate conveyed ideas and react suitably. Indeed, due to its significant nature, it could be argued that listening serves as the bedrock of effective communication.

In order to enhance your listening abilities, it is imperative to acknowledge that active listening necessitates exertion. Artist David Hockney articulates that listening entails a conscientious effort, representing a deliberate and affirmative undertaking.

Prior to providing advice on effective listening skills, let us first determine if you exhibit any characteristics of poor listening habits:

(Extracted from the publication "Power Listening: A Profound Mastery of the Paramount Business Skill", authored by Bernard Ferrari)

The individual known as "The Pretender" exhibits disingenuous engagement in the ongoing conversation while lacking genuine interest in the content shared, as their biases have already determined their stance.

The Opinionator – this poor listener "engages in active listening primarily to evaluate the extent to which others' ideas align with his or her preexisting beliefs."

Individuals who possess an inclination to engage in excessive commentary, often referred to as "Mr. I-Have-an-

Opinion-on-Everything," tend to exhibit the habit of attentively hearing your statements, but consistently respond with counterarguments.

The individual known as the "Solution Man" is unwavering in their determination to find a resolution, even in situations where a collective agreement is lacking within a group.

The individual referred to as "Mr. Pre-Occupied" persistently engages in texting, typing, or engaging in other activities despite being approached for a conversation by another individual. The issue regarding these recipients lies in the uncertainty experienced by individuals regarding the successful delivery of their message or whether they are merely receiving superficial agreement due to the recipient's preoccupation with other tasks.

The Peremptory Listener - this category of poor listener interjects with their own remarks before the speaker has concluded their sentence. This person not only anticipates and completes your sentences, but he also communicates a sense of urgency by stating "Can we expedite this?". This suggests that they prioritize tasks of higher significance over listening to your discourse.

Do you acknowledge any culpability in regards to displaying poor listening skills? If one is desirous of self-improvement, they may consider adhering to these straightforward suggestions:

Focus

Exert your utmost effort in actively listening to the individual with whom you are engaged in conversation. Please bear in mind: there is a distinction between listening and hearing. One might argue that although one may believe they are attentively listening to the individual with whom they are engaged in conversation, if their focus is divided, they are merely perceiving their words rather than fully comprehending their underlying message.

Stop Faking It

Active engagement in the discourse of another individual takes precedence in the act of listening, rather than merely anticipating one's opportunity to speak. Maintain visual contact with the speaker and exhibit appropriate nonverbal cues to acknowledge their communication.

Don't Interrupt

Despite any belief you may hold in the superiority of your viewpoint over that of the individual with whom you are engaged in conversation, it is advised that you allow them to complete their discourse before articulating your own thoughts. Put yourself in his position and you would not welcome being disrupted, hence, do not exhibit impoliteness.

Number four. Reflect

Inevitably, there will arise occasions when you perceive the individual with whom you are conversing as launching personal attacks or purposefully provoking offense. To minimize the occurrence of misinterpretations, it is advisable to pause and engage in self-reflection upon receiving information, prior to responding.

Exercise Awareness of Non-Verbal Signals

Furthermore, aside from giving due consideration to the substance of your message, a crucial aspect of becoming a proficient listener is to be cognizant of the speaker's paralanguage or non-verbal signals. Give regard to the speaker's vocal intonation, facial demeanor, and body language.

Ask Clarification Questions

Despite your intention to listen with utmost attention, there may still exist situations where the message fails to be comprehended fully. Posing inquiries for the purpose of clarification will enhance your comprehension and enable you to provide suitable responses.

7. Empathize

Engaging in empathetic behavior can significantly enhance your capacity to effectively listen. Utilizing this competency entails not merely hearing out an individual, but exerting a sincere endeavor to comprehend and acknowledge their thoughts and viewpoints, even if they diverge from your own. In order to comprehend divergent viewpoints, it is advisable to analyze situations from the perspective of others. An additional approach to demonstrating empathy involves the conscientious examination of circumstances in a neutral and unbiased manner.

Enhancing one's listening abilities is an ongoing process that necessitates substantial dedication and deliberate practice to become a proficient listener. While active listening may not be obligatory in all circumstances, possessing the ability to attentively listen is imperative for becoming a proficient communicator.

Facial Expressions

Your countenance ought to be in harmony with the message you are endeavoring to communicate. The countenances you exhibit ought to epitomize your arguments and effectively engage your audience on an emotional level with the subject matter.

An essential aspect of establishing such a connection lies in utilizing facial expressions that effectively communicate your message to the audience.

It is noteworthy that the human face comprises more than 30 muscles. That's a lot. That implies that your facial expressions possess the capacity to convey a wide range of emotions. It has been postulated that the human countenance exhibits a repertoire of approximately 250,000 distinct expressions. We possess a vast array of expressions at our disposal for the purpose of articulating our sentiments to an audience. The spectators are observing your countenance to gauge the appropriate response to your communication. If you intend to share an amusing anecdote, it would be advisable to precede it with a smile. If the nature of your communication is of a grave nature, then a more somber appearance may be deemed necessary. However, it is essential to maintain a pleasant and congenial facial expression throughout the majority of your presentation. It is advisable to adorn a smile prior to commencing your speech. Approximately 15 facial muscles are involved in the act of smiling. Prior to commencing your speech, ensure to cast a friendly gaze upon the audience, adorned with a warm and welcoming smile.

Gestures

The primary characteristic of a gesture that holds utmost significance is its innate nature. Gestures ought to serve as an organic continuation of the thoughts and verbiage being expressed. Hence, this precludes any form of gesturing that is executed solely for theatrical purposes or meticulously arranged in advance, commonly referred to as choreographed. A gesture inherently lacks inherent meaning; a specific hand gesture does not possess an unequivocal significance. Similar to one's posture, a gesture serves to communicate an impression, occasionally emphasizing a point or implying an emotion. There are, naturally, a few exceptions, one being the gesture of a flat hand used to indicate a request to halt or cease.

Your gesture should be devoid of any cost. Complete liberty should be granted, extending unrestrained from your shoulders down to your fingertips, instead of being confined within the restrictive hold of clenched hands or entangled within folds. A frequent pitfall lies in the tendency for one's elbows to adhere tightly to their sides, while their hands attempt to make graceful gestures, but remain constrained by the restriction around the waist. This behavior is typically caused by feelings of self-consciousness, lack of confidence, or nervousness. As a result, individuals exhibit a peculiar and exaggerated series of arm movements that resemble a windmill rather than natural human gestures.

Another frequent pitfall is the tendency to place the fingertips on the table in front (when standing), or, even worse, keeping them suspended over the buttons of a laptop or mouse, poised to click for the next slide, with only intermittent and brief pauses for a quick gesture, quickly retracting afterwards.

Regardless of your posture, it is essential to ascertain a calm and innate position for your hands, allowing them to function effortlessly. I would suggest that you position your hands in a relaxed manner, finding a resting point that falls between the lower part of your sternum and the upper part of your pelvis when standing, or gently resting them on the table if you are sitting.

Incorporate gesticulations utilizing the arms and hands during conversations to vividly depict events or amplify emphasis. If you maintain a stationary position with your hands firmly fixed at your sides or concealed within your pockets, you will appear inelegant as a presenter. In the context of a presentation, gestures can serve the purpose of extending a warm welcome to the audience, strategically highlighting key points, or subtly signaling the conclusion.

Numerous individuals are uncertain about the appropriate manner in which to position their hands during a speech or presentation. Your hands serve a purpose beyond being mere appendages that should remain concealed. As you engage in the process of learning, it is advisable to utilize all discernible body parts while delivering a speech. This holds particularly true in relation to the utilization of one's upper extremities, including the arms and hands. An effective orator will utilize gestures to occupy the hands and arms, while also aiding in the conveyance of the message to the audience.

We all engage in gesturing, to varying extents among individuals. However, individuals lacking prior experience in public speaking frequently succumb to fear and lose the ability to take action. The hands firmly grasp the podium and do not release their grip. The inability of speakers who are immobilized results in a significant missed opportunity: gestures serve to reinforce one's message and lend additional emphasis to spoken words. Gestures can typically be classified into four discrete domains.

Prompting gestures are additionally utilized in order to facilitate audience compliance with the presenter's instructions. If you desire the approval of the audience, it is imperative that you initiate the act of applause. If you desire the attendees to exhibit participation by raising their hands, then it is incumbent upon you to raise your own hands. You are providing the audience with an illustrative demonstration of the desired conduct.

Bestowing and Receiving Respect

To effectively communicate and influence others, it is imperative to earn their respect. The most uncomplicated means of garnering admiration is through genuinely exhibiting respect. A prevalent misconception among individuals is the confusion between respect and fear. They continuously endeavor to employ actions and tactics that incite fear in others rather than seeking to earn their respect.

The distinction between fear and respect is readily apparent. When an individual holds respect for you, they will make earnest efforts to uphold your values, even when you are not present. However, if an individual solely harbors fear towards you, your values become irrelevant in the absence of your supervision. Establish eye contact frequently and employ their names regularly to impart a sense of significance. Refrain from utilizing your mobile device during the course of your conversation with individuals, and in the event of an imperative telephone call, kindly excuse yourself and ensure to return upon its completion. The level of respect can also be ascertained by evaluating the caliber of the message you communicate to individuals. For instance, a meticulously crafted and polished email yields a greater number of potential opportunities in comparison to a poorly composed communication. The individual perceives the level of effort you invest in editing and writing proficiently, thereby experiencing an automatic sense of respect.

The Virtue of Open-Mindedness: Cultivating a Mindset of Reception

Open-mindedness becomes a crucial part of effective communication. By being receptive, you create an environment that encourages others to share without the concern of divulging excessive details to you. Make a concerted effort to cultivate trust among individuals in regard to the information they disclose to you. Having such an impact enables you to exert influence over them through your words, as they will recognize the extent of your understanding about them as a decisive factor in your choices. Being receptive to different perspectives allows for a deeper comprehension of individuals, thereby refining one's communication abilities to the highest degree.

By harnessing the ability of Empathic Power, one can tap into the strength of Empathy.

Empathy is essentially the trait of comprehending individuals in their true essence. It entails the capacity to comprehend and appropriately respond to individuals' emotional states.

Empathy holds great significance as a crucial social aptitude in the contemporary era. It is crucial to establish a mutual understanding with individuals before they can become receptive to your perspectives or ideas. The impact you will have is contingent upon the level of empathy you demonstrate.

All individuals encounter difficulties when it comes to being comprehended, and irrespective of an individual's position or social standing, there exists a perpetual desire for validation within every human being. It is ingrained in human nature to gravitate towards environments where they feel understood. Therefore, even when faced with difficulties or complexities, individuals would naturally seek solace in your empathetic sanctuary, as you possess a heightened capacity for comprehending their interests. This aspect carries significant importance for fostering a persona of effective leadership. Attaining a promotion would be facilitated by the positive influence you exert upon your superiors within the professional setting.

Develop Strong Interpersonal Relationships through Amicable Interaction

In order to facilitate effective communication, it is imperative to exhibit a certain level of affability. A method of conveying affability to individuals is by engaging them in conversation through the inquiry of personal matters and displaying genuine interest in the details they choose to disclose. Maintaining a consistent smile is also of utmost importance.

A mere display of a smile possesses the power to establish camaraderie amongst individuals unknown to one another, and typically, one's mere presence has the ability to exert influence upon them. An alternative method of demonstrating friendliness is by promoting and fostering individuals to perform at their highest potential, thereby acknowledging and commending their endeavors. Maintaining a demeanor of courtesy proves instrumental in fostering stronger bonds of friendship. In a professional setting, cultivating a wide network of colleagues can significantly expedite and streamline task completion. Productivity flourishes when one nurtures meaningful relationships.

Demonstrate genuine concern for their emotions and exhibit attentiveness to even the smallest particulars. In each and every situation, there exists a universal desire for acknowledgment and gratitude, as it is within this framework that the foundation of companionship is forged.

Be Specific

It is essential to consistently maintain a concise and direct approach, particularly when one is making a request from an individual of great significance. When composing an email, ensure that the subject line captures the essence of the email's objective with an attention-grabbing quality. Minimize the exchange of pleasantries and proceed directly to the explicit intent of the message.

In addition, refrain from circumventing specifics when engaged in discourse concerning matters of significance.

Allocate a specific timeframe for singular discourse, refraining from digressing onto unrelated particulars. To accomplish a particular task, one must channel their attention exclusively towards that objective, minimizing any form of distraction. This will guarantee efficiency across all levels.

Eliminate or eradicate distractions

Identify your sources of distraction and eliminate them. In order to engage in a sustained and uninterrupted dialogue, it is advisable to carefully select a suitable moment when external disturbances are minimized. Please power off your computer and switch your phone to silent mode. The chosen venue must also facilitate undivided focus during your discussion. Additionally, it is imperative to ensure that the counterpart is equally unencumbered by distractions. It is incumbent upon you to furnish all the necessary amenities that will help alleviate any potential distractions.

Power

A competent orator exudes an aura of authority and dominance over the environment by utilizing the potency of their vocal attributes. The primary factor for effectively projecting power from the stage lies in the utilization of volume. Should your vocal volume be insufficient, your message may fail to be audible. Your portrayal will be perceived as lacking strength and efficacy. After a brief passage of time, your audience will cease to engage. Alternatively, excessive volume can swiftly agitate and alienate your audience. You will appear vexed and eager to conclude, akin to an instructive academician. It is universally unfavorable to receive a lecture. The crucial aspect lies in determining an appropriate level of sound amplification that allows for clear audibility among individuals situated towards the rear of the space, while ensuring that those positioned towards the front are not excessively inundated with noise. When utilizing volume, it is important to consider three factors.

Amplitude may be employed in order to accentuate specific aspects that one wishes the audience to retain. As previously stated, the audience remains unaware of the essential points unless deliberate emphasis is placed upon them. A method to accentuate your perspective is by elevating the volume of your voice while introducing the primary elements to the audience.

Reducing your vocal intensity is likewise a highly effective technique for capturing the attention of your audience. When the amplitude of your voice is diminished, it necessitates heightened focus from the audience to comprehend your message. It is particularly suitable when the subject matter is of a grave nature, requiring the audience's full comprehension. Alternatively, it could be deemed suitable in discussions pertaining to matters of sorrow or distress, wherein the intention is to effectively evoke such emotions within the audience. Once more, it is crucial that the audience maintains the ability to audibly comprehend your message.

Voice

The utilization of your voice facilitates varied means of establishing a connection with your audience. It possesses the capacity to adapt and demonstrate significant efficacy. During a presentation, it is advised to employ variations in the volume, pitch, and pace of your voice.

The velocity at which you deliver your presentation greatly influences the degree to which your audience will comprehend and follow it. It might prove challenging for your audience to keep up with your presentation if your speech tempo is excessively slow or fast. Consider modulating the tempo of your delivery to infuse vitality into your presentation. A marginally decelerated segment could convey the notion of vigilance or emphasis, whereas a moderately accelerated presentation can impart a sense of optimism or enthusiasm.

During the process of rehearsing your presentation, experiment with varying the volume, pitch, and pace in order to explore alternative methods of effectively conveying the message intended by a given sentence. Acquaint yourself with your desired vocal registers in order to enhance, express passion, and infuse vitality into the central message of your presentation.

Pace refers to the quantification of one's speaking speed. The peculiarity regarding pacing lies in the fact that it is a commonplace occurrence in our daily discourse. However, for individuals lacking expertise in public speaking, it is swiftly disregarded. The newly appointed speaker dedicates a significant amount of time in the process of collecting relevant materials and concerns themselves with the effective delivery of the message, inadvertently overlooking the aspect of modulating the pace of their spoken words. Inexperienced speakers often exhibit a tendency to speak rapidly, as a result of their nervousness and desire to simply finish their speaking engagements. When one engages in rapid speech, it places a significant burden upon the listeners. You are guiding them through an exploration and they must adhere. If you proceed too swiftly through the material, they may not effectively assimilate all the information being conveyed. By the conclusion of the presentation, they will be fatigued. If you proceed at a sluggish pace, you risk losing your audience to ennui. The brevity of the human attention span renders individuals prone to diverting their focus to matters beyond your own. It should be borne in mind that the human mind has the capacity to comprehend written or spoken words at a faster rate than vocalization permits. A sluggish tempo will lead to the mind becoming distracted and drifting off onto different paths.

Additionally, it is imperative to refrain from delivering your speech with a consistently steady pace, as this can result in a lack of variation and fail to create a sense of dynamism or forward momentum for the audience.

Additionally, it is highly probable that during verbal communication, as one focuses intensively on expressing premeditated ideas, the brain progresses to subsequent thoughts before fully completing the articulation of the initial thought. The outcome entails a perpetual endeavor to keep pace with one's own thoughts, leading to an escalation in speaking tempo.

Nervousness can cause one to speak rapidly and incoherently.

Additionally, speaking rapidly could be a customary behavior that one might be unconsciously exhibiting.

The significance of maintaining a consistent rapid tempo lies in the potential for language to forfeit its inherent rhythm and fluidity, its vibrancy, as well as its capacity to convey precise meaning and establish emphasis. Consequently, it transforms into a monotonous auditory experience, resulting in the disengagement of listeners. Furthermore, should you succeed in upholding this level of intensity, it will undoubtedly prove excessively burdensome for your audience to comprehend the information you are presenting, potentially resulting in their abandonment of any further attempts to engage.

It is imperative to assess your tempo in order to afford the audience adequate time for information assimilation, while simultaneously upholding an unwavering sense of liveliness and vigor in your manner of speech. The alterations in speed are instrumental in preserving the dynamism of language. There will arise occasions wherein it is deemed suitable to engage in a more rapid rate of speech, such as during a transition to a different subject, when inserting a subordinate clause or a casual remark, or even when aiming to express particular emotions such as enthusiasm, imperative, indignation, or apprehension. However, it is equally important to incorporate segments that proceed at a slower tempo, with the intention of highlighting key words, fostering contemplation, and cultivating a sense of intrigue, possibly.

Pace can be employed to engage your audience in the unfolding action. In cinematic productions, as the intensity of the action heightens, the accompanying musical score amplifies in volume and accelerates in tempo. This holds true when participating in an aerobics session. The musical tempo initially begins at a slow pace in order to invigorate blood flow, subsequently accelerating with the intention of encouraging students to increase their speed. The desired outcome can be achieved by increasing the pace of your speech. By controlling the rhythm and tempo of your speech, you can evoke a feeling of anticipation or, propel the audience towards a climactic moment. Incorporating strategically timed and dynamic pacing into your presentation is sure to captivate their attention.

Adopting a decelerated tempo also yields significant benefits. Exercise caution and reduce your pace when approaching certain junctures in your presentation where it is imperative to ensure that your audience effectively comprehends and retains the conveyed information. Once you have effectively captivated your audience through a heightened pace, it may be prudent to decelerate in order to ensure that the intended message is clearly conveyed to those present. Decelerating the tempo can be employed to heighten the dramatic effect of a particular scenario, endowing it with greater significance. It is important to bear in mind that, when approaching a pivotal juncture, significant argument, or climactic moment in the presentation, it is advisable to moderate the pace.

An alternate approach to decelerating the pace is through the utilization of silence. The strategic use of silence can wield significant influence when employed by a skilled orator. The majority of individuals refrain from using it due to their lack of proficiency in its proper application. Silence is often perceived as indicative of frailty or a lack of command by numerous individuals. However, when harnessed skillfully, silence can assume an entirely contrary role. When employing the pregnant pause, it is important to ensure that you maintain engagement with your audience through sustained eye contact to avoid creating the impression that you are mentally disengaged from their presence. A duration of ten to twenty seconds should suffice, but it will be necessary for you to assess and adjust according to the response of the audience. Pacing represents a highly effective technique in the realm of public speaking, and attaining proficiency in its application is within reach.

Consider the content and the intended recipients in your analysis. Highlight the key elements to signify the need for reduced pace in this section. When discussing trivial matters or aiming to create a sense of vigor, accelerate the pace of speech. Regard pacing as an analogous experience to riding a rollercoaster. People partake in rollercoaster rides to experience the thrilling sensations of ascent and descent. Emulate the rollercoaster's pacing. Your presentation ought to encompass both peaks and valleys.

EMPEROR TAROT CARD

The Emperor card signifies the duality of love, offering both solace and torment simultaneously. The higher self of your twin flame holds high expectations for you, spanning across both your professional and personal domains. The Emperor's favor entails a great deal of duty, as it frequently bears implications for one's career, financial matters, or familial obligations intertwined within the bond.

The emperor possesses a deeper understanding and experience of the world, thus embodying a superior social status. Associating oneself with the Emperor entails ascending to a loftier position within the hierarchical structure of society. Should you have ever pondered or harbored aspirations regarding the experience of residing within certain circles of society and enjoying a state of abundant prosperity, you need no longer yearn for it - it shall become your reality. Despite being in a relationship with your twin flame, it does not imply an absolute synchronization of your respective worlds. The Emperor, representing your twin flame, maintains a certain level of guardedness, hindering complete access to their realm. You will consistently find yourself somewhat on the periphery as you refine and develop yourself. Regardless of your personal preference, you shall undergo a profound spiritual awakening, thereby acquiring refined qualities, sophistication, and discernment.

The Emperor represents a state of inherent stability and assurance. No individual is capable of evading the profound depths of the soul's darkness. A spiritual odyssey with the Emperor inevitably entails encountering arduous lessons that deeply resonate with one's soul. Educators in the guise of youngsters, relatives, soul mates, and acquaintances shall manifest to impart valuable teachings concerning matters of the heart. Occasionally, you may find yourself contemplating whether you would have attained greater contentment had you chosen a partner of lesser achievements. The majority of individuals engaging in an Emperor relationship tend to develop a heightened sense of intuition and creativity to effectively cope with the demands and intricacies of the situation.

18

The Emperor bestows material luxuries of the earthly realm, whilst it shall be your duty to bring forth creation. Those who are united with their twin flame, symbolized by the emperor card, will undoubtedly experience the blessings of parenthood, a splendid dwelling, and a prosperous vocation that can only be attained alongside the Emperor. In contemplation of the events that shaped your journey, you shall find yourself reflecting upon the person you once were, in the esteemed presence of the Emperor.

Your accomplishments will undoubtedly instill a sense of pride within you, although a portion of yourself may find solace in reflecting upon whether you have possibly overlooked the most pivotal element of all: establishing a profound connection with your inner spirit. It is imperative to maintain a strong connection in your relationship with your twin flame, as the intensity of this bond can become overwhelming otherwise. In order to endure, it is imperative that one cultivates inner strength, as the counterpart possessing the essence of a regal figure offers worldly consolation while concurrently anticipating solace on an emotional level from you. You are expected to exercise wisdom. It is imperative that you adopt a nurturing attitude towards your twin flame. The Emperor imparts the virtue of fortitude upon you. Your essence will undergo a profound transformation following the bond and subsequent reunion with your twin flame.

The Emperor symbolizes a dynamic wherein your twin flame assumes a position of greater strength, necessitating your individual quest to discover your own distinctive true essence. Ultimately, as your respective roles evolve, you will rise to become the most formidable entity as the wisdom imparted by your twin

flame, the Emperor energy, proves instrumental.

Create An Excellent Initial Impact

The concept of first impressions revolves around the initial assessments we make upon establishing a connection with an unfamiliar individual. These conclusions are established on the basis of the individual's demeanor, linguistic expression, sartorial choices, as well as a wide range of factors encompassing both ambiguous and superficial aspects, along with profound and intuitive elements.

In order to gain a satisfactory level of comprehension about an individual, it is necessary to allocate a substantial amount of time in their company. It is highly unlikely that a person of sound judgment would make a complete assessment of an individual solely based on their initial impression. However, there are instances in life where it becomes vitally important to quickly captivate and impress one's audience. Initial perceptions do not delay or inquire into the reasons before forming conclusions. Unbeknownst to us, the intricate mechanisms at play in our initial perceptions of individuals allow our cognition to construct a comprehensive representation of their anticipated qualities.

While perusing this chapter, kindly keep in mind that establishing a favorable initial perception hinges upon the genuine expression of your true essence. Initial opinions are prone to being largely influenced by various superficial attributes. When we are at ease and experience a sense of belonging, we have a natural inclination to project a positive initial impression without much effort.

It is not anticipated that one would acquire profound understanding of your innermost being during initial encounters; therefore, the primary objective is to exhibit genuineness. This can manifest itself through the demonstration of courteousness, engagement, and self-assurance. Individuals possess a keen ability to discern insincere conduct, and the most guaranteed means to undermine your initial impression is by projecting an artificial persona. An initial impression does not present an opportunity for self-promotion; rather, it offers an occasion for individuals to gradually become acquainted and foster mutual rapport.

Developing a Favorable Initial Impression during a Job Interview

People swiftly develop impressions of you within moments. During an interview, it is essential to overcome any nervousness and let your true personality radiate. A significant proportion of corporate HR managers and small business owners openly acknowledge prioritizing cultural alignment over professional expertise in their recruitment processes. Given the high volume of applications that job postings typically attract, establishing rapport during the interview process can greatly enhance one's prospects. If the interviewer perceives you as a highly compatible candidate, your likelihood of securing the job may surpass that of another individual with greater qualifications. If a congenial discussion transpires, and they ascertain your commitment to acquiring the requisite proficiencies for the position, there is a higher probability that you will be advanced through the subsequent stages of the recruitment procedure.

Irrespective of the level of tension you may be experiencing, endeavor to seek methods of relaxation that do not appear nonchalant. If the individual conducting the interview is your prospective employer, it is probable that their expertise lies not in the realm of interviewing but in their respective area of specialization. Unless you are being interviewed by a seasoned professional like Oprah, it is prudent to assume that the interviewer may possess a modicum of uncertainty regarding their proficiency in this particular field. They might conduct only a limited number of interviews annually and are inclined to ask standardized questions due to the absence of scientific methodologies in this regard. The majority of individuals who engage in interviews often experience a degree of uneasiness in performing this task. Remain genuine and exhibit your true character as you strive to acquire comprehensive knowledge about your interviewer.

Adhere to these guidelines in order to excel in your upcoming interview:

1. Concentrate on the Interviewer

Direct your attention to the interviewer as they assume utmost significance during that particular instance. It is imperative that you bestow upon them your full and undivided attention. Exercise caution in not prematurely promoting yourself by prioritizing speaking over active listening. Demonstrate sincere interest in securing the position.

One can inquire directly with the interviewer as to the key aspects of the job description that hold the highest priority. Pay attention to the entirety of their requirements. In order to evince your attentiveness, endeavor to pose inquiries that are tailored to each requirement and elicit supplementary information. Engaging them in conversation regarding their company will enhance their level of comfort towards you. This presents an exceptional occasion to acquire further insights into the role you are seeking. It is imperative to maintain consistent vigilance for possible warning signs, as such indicators can serve as valuable inquiries to be posed at a later time.

Now that you have insight into their requirements, proceed to present the aptitudes, expertise, and attributes you possess that align with their expectations. Exercise discretion when engaging in conversations about areas of limited experience. There is no necessity for you to openly admit your shortcomings, nevertheless, it is imperative to convey your assurance in your ability to acquire any skills that you may not currently feel completely at ease with. It's all about authenticity. Ensure to display positive body language, establish consistent eye contact, and appropriately use facial expressions such as smiling. Adhere to sustained visual engagement throughout the interview, regardless of whether it takes place online or in a physical setting. This demonstrates your assurance and attentiveness towards their remarks.

2. Keep Your Composure

Ensure you maintain a proper posture and convey genuine engagement with each of the interviewers. Make an effort to avoid getting disoriented, losing focus, or feeling camera timid. I appreciate the adage of maintaining composure in adverse situations. Stay focused.

One can derive comfort in knowing that the interviewer shares an equal level of concern in selecting the most suitable candidate for the position. In the event of an onsite interview, it is advisable to maintain an upright posture, refrain from slouching, retract your shoulders, and display composure during the entire session. In the event that you become aware of any fidgeting tendencies, exert control over them while avoiding excessive analysis. Displaying unfavorable physical gestures will not compromise your chances of securing the position, however fixating on any adverse self-perception could undermine an otherwise exceptional interview. Remember, the only reason you could have been invited to the interview is that you are very likely the best person for the job.

When participating in a video interview, ensure that the audio, lighting, and video clarity are all of exceptional quality. The background ought to possess a tidy and well-ordered appearance that mirrors one's personality. Please ensure that you activate the camera prior to logging in to ensure that you are properly illuminated and that there are no potential distractions within the camera's frame. Ensure that all individuals in your vicinity are adequately informed about the ongoing circumstances in order to reduce the likelihood of any form of disruption or diversion. In the event of an interruption occurring during the interview, it presents a valuable occasion for you to demonstrate your ability to handle unexpected situations and adapt accordingly to your interviewer. Maintain your composure, stay attentive, and exhibit a courteous demeanor.

3. Ask Questions

It would be prudent for you to enter the interview equipped with a set of inquiries meticulously crafted based on the extensive research you have conducted regarding both the company and the position.

To establish rapport, you may direct your initial inquiry towards the interviewer. One could inquire about their reasons for opting to join said company and inquire as to what aspects of its culture they find most appealing. Discover their sources of job satisfaction or ascertain what aspects of their work bring them joy. Inquire as to whether they possess any counsel they could offer to an individual in your current circumstance, embarking on their journey with the organization.

4. Reflect Your Interviewer's Behavior

Adapting to your interviewer's communication style can facilitate the conversation. Individuals communicate using various methods; certain individuals engage in direct and rapid conversations, while others prefer a more deliberate and unhurried speaking style. Pay attention to the interviewer's rhythm and mirror it in your responses.

In the event that your interviewer communicates with a deliberate and articulate manner, it is advisable to adopt a similar approach. This will create the perception that they have encountered an individual who shares similarities, fostering a sense of ease and comfort within them. Repeating or echoing speech patterns is an understated means of signaling concurrence and a readiness to find middle ground. It would be advisable to contemplate the occasional utilization of their name during the interview. When an individual's name is brought up during a conversation, they often exhibit a noticeable level of engagement and responsiveness. It captivates their focus and nurtures a feeling of closeness. Referring to individuals by their name can be impactful, yet it is imperative to exercise moderation.

Mirroring, or isopraxism as it is sometimes referred to, constitutes a form of imitation. We engage in reciprocal mimicry as a means of providing solace and reassurance to each other—this behavior is observable not only among humans but also certain members of the animal kingdom. Individuals have the ability to develop connections and foster reliance through the synchronization of their speech patterns, body language, vocabulary, and tone, all of which occur inadvertently. One is seldom conscious of this behavior until someone astutely observes the striking similarity between the manner in which they carry themselves while conversing with a novel acquaintance, and the posture they assume when engaging in discourse with a close companion during a social gathering.

The captivating nature of this occurrence can be attributed to a fundamental principle in biology, namely aversion to the unfamiliar and attraction to the familiar. The aforementioned principle is applicable to our affinity towards individuals and notions that bear resemblance. This instills a sense of security within us, as we are well-aware of the nature of our interactions with individuals who possess similar principles.

Avoiding Interruption

It is generally disliked when individuals experience interruptions. We have all encountered individuals at some juncture who possess the inability to allow another person to complete a sentence. Their intention is to anticipate and provide the word you are attempting to convey prior to its utterance. Alternatively, individuals may interrupt to express their own viewpoints or recount a personal anecdote that surpasses the significance of what others wish to communicate. Interrupting is not only impolite; it engenders reluctance in individuals to engage in conversation with someone who consistently interrupts.

Should you be perusing this and happen to possess a proclivity for chronic interruption, rest assured. This chapter explores both facets of the situation. Strategies for handling interruptions and techniques for overcoming the tendency to interrupt individuals. Incorporating perspectives from both parties is the optimal strategy to mitigate disruptions across all domains of communication.

Breaking a habit requires patience and mindfulness. The majority of research has indicated that the typical duration for establishing or eradicating a habit is ninety days, a period of time that, when considered in the broader context, is relatively short. Particularly when the temporal and exerted endeavors can significantly enhance one's skills in communication.

The initial step in discontinuing the habit of interrupting entails diligently focusing on individuals during a discourse. Please consult the section dedicated to active listening within the chapter for further elaboration on this topic. The act of interruption often arises when an individual is contemplating their forthcoming statement while another person is speaking. This indicates a lack of attentiveness on their part, as they tend to interject their thoughts prior to the individual completing their statement.

In order to cease this, it is imperative that you allocate your undivided attention to someone. Exhibit attentiveness and actively engage in attentive listening when conversing with others. Pay heed to their words. Once the individual has concluded their remarks, construct your response and offer a reply. Initially, this task may present challenges due to the significant level of mindfulness required. If one has established a reputation for interruption and is conscious of this tendency, it is highly likely that others will perceive an increased level of attentiveness towards them.

This subject matter also pertains to the domain of persistent problem resolution. Attempting to resolve an issue in the absence of its existence poses a significant challenge for individuals who engage in interruption. I readily acknowledge and take full responsibility for engaging in this behavior, particularly in relation to my spouse. She will be imparting information to me, upon which my natural inclination will be to infer an issue requiring my intervention. I find satisfaction in resolving challenges, yet interjecting while she is speaking to contribute my viewpoint often leads to unfavorable outcomes.

The subsequent course of action involves exercising patience. Take a breath. This aligns with the initial aspect of breaking the habit. Upon concluding the conversation, pause briefly, allow a few moments to lapse, and subsequently provide a response. There is no imperative for an immediate response and to progress through the conversation rapidly, resembling the forceful progression of a freight train. Exercising patience affords you the opportunity to cultivate the most optimal response possible. Additionally, it allows the interlocutor an opportunity to supplement their response if deemed necessary.

An alternate manner of interjecting, which is both unwelcome and typically met with unfavorable response, is intruding upon a conversation between others. Two individuals are engaged in conversation, when an individual elected to interject their perspective and provide unsolicited counsel. There is no justification for interjecting unless one has something constructive to contribute or a means to enhance the conversation.

Ultimately, should you find yourself constantly being interrupted during your discourse, how would this affect your emotional state? Adopt an alternative viewpoint and genuinely consider the perspective that another individual would experience. As is evident, one does not experience a state of wellness. When considering this issue from the standpoint of the individual who is being interrupted, it can be likened to the abrupt imposition of a stop sign that forcefully halts their discourse. Not a good feeling.

Responding to Interruption

Now, let us proceed to discuss the appropriate manner of managing interruptions as and when they arise.

Preventing interruption completely is an unattainable objective; interruptions are inevitable. Occasionally, it is advisable to relinquish one's attachment and react in a suitable manner. Reacting angrily in response to an interruption is a highly counterproductive approach that tends to exacerbate the frequency of interruptions.

Disregarding an interruption and allowing the individual to speak can be considered the optimal course of action at times. If an individual displays an overwhelming enthusiasm for speaking that renders them difficult to interrupt, it is advised to allow them to express their thoughts and subsequently resume the prior discussion. Perhaps the individual disrupting the conversation possesses a viewpoint or insight that they perceive as being essential, and they exhibit eagerness in contributing it. It would be prudent to accord them the opportunity to express their thoughts. You will soon regain your equilibrium.

Kindly inform individuals that you will require additional time. This is advantageous when commencing a presentation or a class. When conducting a lecture in a professional setting, I will kindly request all participants to withhold their questions until the conclusion of the session. By engaging in this action, I establish clear and defined expectations for the collective. If someone interrupts by posing a question, my response will vary depending on the stage of my presentation. I might opt to state, "I will address that matter momentarily," or "I shall provide an answer to your query shortly, but allow me to conclude this segment first." The responses I offer are concise, straightforward, and devoid of any impoliteness.

Disregarding an interruption is an alternative approach to manage the situation. I have been in the midst of sharing a narrative, and on occasions when someone interjects, I will persist in my discourse. This train will not make any stops for anyone. If you adopt this approach, it may necessitate amplifying the projection of your voice. Please note that the approach I am about to describe is relatively assertive compared to the alternative methods I have previously suggested. This could potentially result in the other individual exhibiting similar behavior, potentially including a heightened rate of speech. When considering the utilization of this approach, it is advisable to assess the circumstances and question whether engaging in this conflict is a worthwhile endeavor.

In certain instances, adopting a direct approach is the most effective means of managing interruption. Kindly notify the individual that you found their interruption to be disrespectful. This can prove beneficial for individuals who frequently engage in the act of interruption. In the event that an individual repeatedly interjects during an ongoing conversation. Kindly reply with a statement such as, "This marks the __ occasion in which you have interrupted me. I kindly request that you allow me to conclude my thoughts before intervening." It is possible that the individual who is interrupting may not be fully aware of the extent to which they engage in interruptions. Employing this assertion would have a similar effect as dousing them with liquid. They will acquire an understanding of their actions, particularly if they have been consistently interrupting individuals over an extended period of time.

The final alternative is to endeavor to ascertain the underlying reasons behind the individual's act of interruption. They might possess information of considerable significance to convey to you. Observe the current circumstances; do they exhibit signs of nervousness? If they display signs of concern, it is possible that an urgent issue has arisen, and they should duly apprise you of it. Inquire about the ongoing matter and endeavor to ascertain the underlying reasons for their interruptions. Now, the scenario depicted is primarily aligned with a work setting, yet the underlying principle remains consistent. Determine the reason for their interruption and proceed accordingly.

A myriad of approaches have been proffered herein, elucidating the means by which interruptions may be effectively managed. In addition to directly attending to the disruption, these approaches exhibit non-aggressive characteristics. I have employed all of these approaches. From my perspective, disregarding the interruption and proceeding with the conversation is the strategy I tend to favor. Indeed, each of these examples carries potential utility. Hence, it is advisable to assess the prevailing circumstances comprehensively before proceeding. The exercises provided in this chapter offer alternatives for practicing each of these methods with a partner, should you prefer not to employ them publicly immediately.

Exercise #8.1

How to stop interrupting. Please examine the techniques outlined in the introductory section of this chapter. The initial step involves making a deliberate effort to acknowledge and recognize that you possess a tendency to interrupt. In the event that you become aware of an impending interruption, exert effort to prevent it from occurring. Make an effort to provide the individual you are conversing with undivided attention. Please exercise restraint for a brief period after their discourse concludes before offering your input.

Subsequently, in the event of an inadvertent interruption, it is advisable to engage in retrospective consideration at a later time. Consider it from their point of view. How did it feel to experience an interruption caused by your actions? Gaining insight from their viewpoint will enhance your comprehension and aid in preventing its recurrence.

An effective method for honing this skill in collaboration with a partner entails engaging in dialogue with them and refining the synchronization. Following their speech, kindly allow a brief pause of two seconds before giving your response. This process will facilitate your critical examination of your responses and foster a heightened sense of attentiveness towards others during conversations.

Exercise #8.2

Methods to mitigate interruptions. Please carefully examine and evaluate all of the approaches that have been discussed in the second section of this chapter. The aforementioned approaches can be classified as a selective approach to handling interruptions. Disregarding it was the initial approach, and at times, that might be the most suitable course of action depending on the circumstances. Work meetings are usually full of interruptions, and unless your point is crucial, let it go, or try and repeat it later.

Let people know that you will be speaking for quite some time and to hold off questions till the end. This is an excellent way to start a presentation because it sets your expectations of how the group will behave.

Disregarding the interruption is an approach to addressing it. This technique can be readily implemented with the assistance of an individual. Collaborate with a colleague and ask them to endeavor at interrupting you while you are speaking. Endeavor to amplify your speaking volume and articulate assertively. Kindly request that they refrain from interrupting while you speak assertively with an elevated volume.

The act of expressing oneself in a straightforward manner can evoke feelings of extreme fear. However, on certain occasions, it becomes the most suitable course of action, particularly when an individual has persistently and incessantly disrupted one's train of thought over a prolonged period. Certainly, if addressing individuals for their tendency to interrupt is deemed excessive at this juncture, it would be advisable to collaborate with a colleague instead. Similar to the physical activity mentioned in the preceding passage. Commence speaking while allowing your partner to interject. When they exhibit a direct approach. Kindly allow me to conclude before you respond. Any response that effectively conveys this message will suffice.

Ultimately, uncover the reason behind their act of interruption. Analyze the circumstances and ascertain the cause of the individual's interruption. This can be executed in conjunction with a collaborator. Initiate conversation and allow for their interjections. Cease the interruption and inquire in a manner such as, "Do you have a matter of urgency to convey, pray tell?" Employing this approach is akin to being forthright while affording the interrupter an opportunity to communicate should they possess a genuine need to express themselves.

Fostering Empathy In A Professional Environment To Cultivate A Deeper Understanding Of Colleagues

Empathy can be likened to a versatile and multipurpose cleansing agent. When there is the presence of empathy, every problem has the potential to be resolved.

An essential competency required for this role is the capacity to understand and interpret the emotions of individuals. We have the ability to leverage technology in order to resolve conflicts, foster highly efficient teams, and augment our engagement with colleagues, customers, and clientele.

Nonetheless, the vast majority of individuals within our community exhibit a strong sense of self-assurance regarding their capacity to acquire new technical proficiencies. However, there exists a collective sentiment of inadequacy when it comes to enhancing our interpersonal aptitudes. And a lot of individuals are embarrassed to talk about their sentiments, let alone those of others!

This chapter elucidates the essence of empathy. We will explore the potential enhancement of interpersonal relationships, promotion of an atmosphere characterized by transparency and candor, and the consequential positive effects on the mental well-being and efficacy of our colleagues, by implementing a set of uncomplicated measures.

In this chapter, it is my intention to offer a reiterated definition of empathy in relation to the subject matter at hand. In its most rudimentary iteration, empathy refers to the ability to discern and comprehend the emotions of others, as well as grasp their perspectives on a given situation. At its utmost level, empathy enables individuals to utilize that comprehension in order to uplift another person's morale and provide assistance in navigating challenging situations.

Whilst they may bear distinction, compassion and empathy are occasionally perceived incorrectly. When someone requires your attention, it is possible to perceive that attending to their needs could potentially increase their overall happiness. As opposed to empathy, sympathy does not encompass a comparable perspective or range of emotions.

In the absence of prior knowledge of their circumstances, one might experience a sense of empathy towards an individual observed weeping in a public setting. While it is not imperative, empathy has the potential to develop from sympathy.

Daniel Goleman, a highly esteemed psychologist, enumerates empathy as one of the fundamental components of emotional intelligence, an indispensable attribute for effective leadership. Its development can be categorized into three stages: compassionate empathy, emotional empathy, and cognitive empathy. Subsequently, we will proceed to discuss each level consecutively.

Mental Empathy

The concept of comprehending the thoughts or emotions of another individual is referred to as cognitive or mental empathy. The observer is not required to emotionally engage.

Cognitive empathy enables managers to gain a comprehensive understanding of their team members' experiences, thereby facilitating the identification of appropriate leadership strategies that would be most effective in the present circumstances. Moreover, sales representatives can make use of this tool to ascertain the customer's emotional state, consequently allowing them to choose the most effective approach for communication.

The aptitude for cognitive empathy predominantly relies on rationality, cerebral reasoning, and emotional detachment. This suggests that certain individuals engage in its misuse. One example of how a person exhibiting Machiavellian personality traits might utilize cognitive empathy is by manipulating an individual who possesses emotional vulnerability.

Emotional Empathy

The aptitude for emotional empathy enabled an individual to gain a deeper understanding of another person, as they possess the ability to empathize with and connect to their emotions. Due to its impact or modification of oneself, it is often denoted as "affective empathy." Understanding an individual's emotions holds significance, alongside the establishment of a genuine rapport with them.

This level of empathy might exceed the capacity of individuals to manage. Individuals with a high degree of empathy often find themselves emotionally entangled in the concerns or distress of others, occasionally compromising their own emotional well-being. This holds particularly true in instances where they lack the necessary capabilities to navigate the situation.

Through the implementation of brief breaks, the careful evaluation of personal limits, and the enhancement of one's ability to manage the demands associated with this specific role, the occurrence of emotional exhaustion stemming from excessive benevolence can be effectively averted.

Individuals in positions of leadership would benefit from obtaining a fundamental understanding of emotional empathy. It promotes a culture of integrity and openness, facilitating the cultivation of strong trust and open communication between supervisors and subordinates. However, the combination of empathy and action proves to be highly beneficial.

Kindhearted Empathy

Compassionate empathy stands out as the most dynamically engaged form of empathy. It involves not only demonstrating empathy and comprehending the anguish of another individual but also taking tangible actions to alleviate it.

Consider, for example, the scenario where one of your team members expresses dissatisfaction and becomes upset following an unsuccessful presentation. Recognizing their anguish holds significance, and it carries even greater significance to affirm their reaction by exhibiting indications of the identical sentiments. One of the most significant actions one can undertake on their behalf is to allocate a portion of their time in order to offer guidance or support that will aid them in overcoming the issue and preparing for future challenges.

How to Cultivate Compassion within the Workplace

Initially, you may encounter some difficulty in expressing empathy due to a sense of hesitation or a perceived inability to emotionally invest. However, you are not predetermined to experience failure due to this.

In order to effectively employ empathy, it is imperative to relinquish your own perspective and earnestly consider matters from the other person's standpoint. Upon comprehending that an individual's behavior is essentially a response rooted in their prior learning and encounters, one can discern actions that initially seem excessively emotional, stubborn, or irrational.

The subsequent strategies ought to be consistently employed to the extent that they become ingrained.

Pay Complete Attention

Exercise acute attentiveness to the message being conveyed by an individual. In order to fully grasp the meaning they intend to convey, employ your auditory faculties, visual perception, and intuitive instincts.

Begin by giving careful consideration to the crucial vocabulary and expressions that they utilize, particularly if they do so with regularity. Subsequently, contemplate the manner in which they articulate their thoughts as well as the intended message underlying their words. What is the impression you perceive from their tone or demeanor? As an illustration, do they exhibit feelings of intense anger, deep humiliation, or profound fear?

To further enhance one's understanding and demonstrate empathy, it is imperative to engage in active listening. At this juncture, kindly abstain from posing direct inquiries, expressing disagreement with the current discourse, or presenting valid areas of disagreement. Moreover, it is crucial to maintain a versatile mindset and be prepared for the conversation to deviate from its intended course as the other individual's perspectives and emotions may fluctuate.

Consider the viewpoints of others

You may be familiar with the popular proverb "To truly understand and evaluate an individual, it is advisable to empathetically experience their circumstances by walking a mile in their shoes." Evaluate your mindset and sustain a receptive mental perspective. Excessive emphasis on one's presumptions and opinions restricts the opportunity for empathetic understanding.

After gaining an understanding of the reasoning behind others' perspectives, you have the ability to embrace any standpoint. While it is not necessary for you to agree with it, it is currently not an opportune moment for us to engage in a discussion. Rather, ensure a focused and respectful approach by attentively listening and treating them courteously.

In situations of uncertainty, it is advisable to seek clarification from the individual regarding their viewpoint, and subsequently inquire about any potential resolutions they may suggest for addressing the issue. The most efficient and direct approach to understanding another individual typically involves inquiring the relevant inquiries.

Do Something
There is no definitive approach to demonstrating compassion and empathy. The outcome will be contingent upon the specific conditions, the individual involved, and the prevailing sentiment in the given moment. It is important to bear in mind that empathy entails prioritizing the wants and needs of others above your own. Therefore, every action you undertake or suggestion you propose

should aim to bring about benefits specifically for them.

As an illustration, it is plausible that one of your team members might be experiencing distractions within their household environment, thereby presenting challenges to their ability to maintain focus on their assigned tasks. Informing them that they have the opportunity to work remotely until the situation is resolved may be perceived as benevolent; however, continued employment could potentially offer them a constructive diversion from distressing contemplations. Therefore, inquire as to their preference regarding the preferred strategy.

Additionally, it is important to note that empathy should not be limited to times of necessity. Having the ability to perceive situations from various perspectives is a valuable asset that can be utilized consistently and in any given situation. Spontaneous acts of kindness have the power to enhance the well-being of individuals.

Empathy is exemplified, as an example, through the act of smiling and conscientiously recalling individuals' names. Exemplifying empathetic behavior encompasses actively listening to individuals during meetings, displaying genuine curiosity about their personal pursuits, and delivering constructive feedback that proves valuable.

Use these abilities frequently. You will establish a commendable image as a benevolent and reliable individual, demonstrating an inclination towards acknowledging and understanding the perspectives, emotions, and encounters of others. This will contribute significantly to your role as a valuable asset to both your team and the overall success of the company.

In conclusion and for purposes of summary

Empathy entails the ability to recognize and comprehend the emotions of others as well as to gain insight into their perspectives. It constitutes as one of the quintessential constituents of emotional intelligence, fostering the establishment of stable relationships and the cultivation of trust.

Existence of Three Phases of Empathy:

Gaining insight into an individual's emotional state necessitates the employment of cognitive empathy.

Participating in and transmitting these sentiments constitutes emotional empathy.

Empathy and compassion necessitate taking action to provide assistance to others.

Fully focus on your colleague, actively observing their verbal and nonverbal cues to thoroughly understand their situation, thereby exhibiting empathy. Put aside any preconceived notions you may have, maintain a receptive attitude towards your colleague's emotions, foster an emotional bond, and subsequently implement measures to bolster their welfare.

Conquer Unfavorable Behaviors

Each cognitive process, behavioral act, or emotional experience elicits subtle modifications within the brain. As previously stated, with frequent repetition, an activity transforms into a habitual behavior. Some individuals possess commendable attributes, whereas others lack desirable qualities. Irrespective of its nature, modifying habits is a formidable task, yet attainable through deliberate exertion. Having become acquainted with the habit loop, it is now imperative to comprehend the process of altering specific habits. Provided herein is a straightforward illustration for your contemplation.

As an illustration, Adam opts to visit Starbucks in order to socialize with his acquaintances rather than engage in studying activities at the library. He is aware that in order to sustain his academic performance, he must allocate several hours each day to studying. Nonetheless, engaging in social activities and enjoying the company of his friends brings him joy. The objective in this context is to assist in the implementation of a structured regimen that allows him to dedicate more time to his studies while still experiencing the same sense of joy derived from socializing with his peers. What can he do? An alternative approach could involve dedicating a period of solitary study, with the notion of socializing serving as a form of incentive or reward for diligent academic efforts. An alternative course of action would involve his convening with his acquaintances at the library for the purpose of studying, and subsequently indulging himself at Starbucks.

In both instances, Adam is strategically attempting to modify the habitual sequence and the associated gratification elements of the habit loop. It entails interrupting the sequence of cues, routines, and rewards associated with visiting Starbucks or socializing with his friends. Let us examine the habit cycle from an alternative standpoint. For example, if you endeavor to relinquish the tendency to incessantly rectify others during conversational exchanges. The prevailing indicator in the given scenario is the presence of another individual engaging in conversation, wherein your observation reveals the utterance of an erroneous statement. The procedure is rectifying the individual in question. The gratification lies in knowing that you have successfully rectified the other individual's mistake, resulting in an improved state of well-being. Presently, the moment has arrived to liberate oneself from this routine.

The initial action entails interrupting the cue. Therefore, whenever an individual utters an erroneous statement or commits an error, you have the alternative to either rectify their misconception or choose to disregard it. In order to surmount the tendency to rectify others, it is imperative to direct one's attention towards conscious cogitations at the outset. You will have to consciously stop yourself from correcting others because you will not gain anything from it. After interrupting the cue, you can proceed to establish a different pattern of engaging as an attentive listener. Rather than attempting to rectify their mistakes, it is advisable to attentively listen to the content they wish to convey. In conclusion, the potential benefits include enhanced communication with others which may facilitate the development of professional connections and social engagement.

In order to liberate oneself from a habit, one must analyze the triggering stimulus, the established pattern, and the subsequent gratification. This provides a deeper understanding of your behaviors, facilitating their modification.

Nevertheless, it is imperative to grasp the concept that every habit adheres to a specific formula or pattern dictated by the mind in an automated manner. To establish a novel pattern of behavior, it is necessary to restructure the current sequence of steps. One cannot abruptly terminate a habitual behavior. Alternatively, you will need to generate a substitute for it. Commence by determining the behavior you wish to modify. Subsequently, proceed to discern the stimulus that initiates it, the sequence of actions you undertake, and the benefit you achieve.

Pitfalls to Avoid

Regarding the alteration of a habit, it necessitates a deliberate exertion of willpower and a steadfast commitment to regularity. The incorporation of repetition plays a significant role in fostering the adherence of a newly formed habit. In order to uphold a state of physical well-being, it is imperative to anticipate any potential obstacles that may arise while adhering to wholesome routines. Presented below are several prevalent errors often encountered during the process of cultivating positive behavior patterns.

Simultaneously Performing All Tasks
In order to establish a novel routine, it will be necessary for you to compile a comprehensive inventory of the behaviors or skills that you aspire to modify or acquire. In the early stages, you may possess the determination to achieve success. Over time, the demands and obligations of daily life become increasingly burdensome, and the desire to revert to previous behaviors is elicited. In due course, the experience of being inundated precipitates a gradual regression to former behavioral tendencies. As an illustration, it may be advisable to engage in regular physical

activity. You have made the decision to engage in a one-hour exercise routine at the early hour of 5 a.m. daily. You adhere to the schedule for a few days, but eventually relinquish your commitment due to its failure in providing sufficient opportunity for rest and recuperation. Alternatively, it is conceivable that the timetable has grown excessively demanding, rendering you unable to adhere to it. When seeking to alter a habit, it is imperative to place emphasis on fostering long-term sustainability in the process of transformation. This can be accomplished by selecting a single task and executing it with precision.

In search of a noteworthy beginning

Initiating a novel routine can be quite challenging. Whenever one endeavors to promptly accomplish a task through exerting immense effort, it merely serves to exacerbate the level of difficulty. By engaging in this action, you are essentially positioning yourself for inevitable disappointment. Let us contemplate the scenario wherein you are cultivating a routine of engaging in exercise on a consistent basis. At the outset, it is possible that you will be able to engage in physical exercise for a duration of one to two hours on a daily basis. After a span of seven days, it becomes apparent that you are unable to allocate this substantial amount of time to your physical fitness routine. Ultimately, you relinquish the pursuit of physical exercise entirely. A significant portion of the population eventually finds themselves in similar circumstances.

When it concerns the cultivation of a habit, direct your attention towards commencing with modest and achievable tasks. It primarily involves familiarizing oneself with the routine and consistently executing it, rather than fixating on the duration expended in doing so. If one wishes to establish a routine of regular physical activity, it is imperative to grasp the concept that the initial action required is simply to commence engaging in exercise. The specific duration, be it 10 minutes or an hour, holds no significance. Please make certain that you engage in physical activity each day without exception. A duration of 10 minutes may appear inconsequential, and the prospect of sustaining it may not seem unduly arduous. This is precisely the course of action that must be undertaken. Instead of seeking an extravagant beginning, initiate small-scale endeavors. When faced with a seemingly effortless change, the probability of declining such modification diminishes inherently. Consequently, this facilitates the process of ensuring the habit becomes ingrained.

Exhibit Awareness towards the Environment

The environment is a crucial factor in facilitating habit change and ensuring its sustainability. Behaviors constitute an integral component of both your tangible and interpersonal surroundings. As an illustration, the scent emitted by food serves as a prompt to assume a seated position and consume it. Likewise, the sight of the television upon returning home from work can serve as a signal to relax and destress. You can harness the power of the surroundings to facilitate the formation of a lasting habit. For example, adorning a wall with motivational posters or employing sticky notes containing inspirational quotes can yield advantageous outcomes. Engaging in conversations with your acquaintances, relatives, and associates regarding your objectives serves as a means of reinforcement to maintain your focus.

Summary

Allow us to expeditiously outline the salient points that have been deliberated upon in this chapter:

In order to improve your communication skills, you will need to address any bad habits that you may have created.

Habits become ingrained in our neural pathways through the consistent repetition of an activity; once established, these habitual processes can be executed effortlessly, free from conscious deliberation.

The habit loop is comprised of three distinct phases: (1) the initiation cue, (2) the behavioral response, and (3) the consequential reward.

During a conversation, numerous prevalent detrimental behaviors can occur, such as diverting attention to one's phone or habitually interrupting others. These undesirable habits significantly hinder one's capacity to establish meaningful connections with other individuals.

In order to surmount an undesirable tendency, it is imperative to cultivate self-awareness regarding the behavioral patterns one is manifesting. Upon identifying a habit that necessitates rectification, it becomes necessary to dislodge the habitual loop and substitute it with a revised one.

Communication In Relationships

Strong interpersonal relationships are established based on multiple factors, with open communication being among them. Insufficient transparent communication between individuals and their loved ones may lead to potential discord in their relationships. It is of utmost importance to prioritize active listening and mindful communication during these discussions.

In this chapter, we will examine the most appropriate communication styles for effectively addressing various relationships, encompassing your partner, parents, acquaintances, and offspring, should they be present. Each section will explore the four attributes of proficient communication and their practical applicability.

Significant Other

If you happen to be involved in a healthy and fulfilling partnership, it is highly likely that engaging in discussions and exchanges with your significant other tends to flow effortlessly and naturally. It is highly probable that you mutually comprehend one another effortlessly on the majority of occasions, and it is likely that conversing in a casual manner poses no difficulty whatsoever. Ordinary discourse within such relationships generally tends to be uncomplicated.

What if you have a matter of great significance to address? In the event that you are dissatisfied with a particular facet of your relationship or your overall life circumstances, what options could be explored? If one is contemplating significant changes and envisioning future aspirations, how might they engage in a discussion with their spouse or significant other regarding these matters?

Engaging in these dialogues may pose greater difficulty. It is imperative to ensure that the intended message is unambiguous and comprehensible, allowing your beloved individual to grasp your perspective and intentions. It is imperative to ensure that no emotional harm is inflicted and a comprehensive understanding of your intended message is achieved. This is the point at which proficient communication abilities truly manifest themselves.

Word Choice

It is crucial to exercise caution in selecting one's words when engaging in substantive discussions with one's spouse or partner. It is imperative to ensure that they comprehend the intended message without causing any emotional distress or conveying unwarranted blame.

It is highly likely that if there is a significant matter you wish to address with your beloved, you have likely pondered it extensively. Allocate additional time to mentally rehearse the dialogue. Consider alternative approaches to express your intended message and attempt to envision their potential reactions. Continuously rehearse the dialogue until you attain a level of ease to engage in it.

There is no compulsion to engage in verbalized rehearsals for this exercise, nor is it necessary to allocate dedicated time for its completion. One can engage in mental rehearsals of possible conversations while simultaneously performing household chores or driving. You are neglecting the method of articulation and solely fixating on the content of your message. This can be accomplished entirely within one's thoughts, alleviating any feelings of self-consciousness that may arise from speaking aloud in front of a mirror.

Tone

Should you find yourself with a significant matter to broach with your partner, it is probable that you are experiencing heightened emotional sentiments in relation to said matter. It is acceptable to express such emotions to your partner; however, it is important to be mindful of your vocal inflection. Please refrain from raising your voice to a level that could be interpreted as yelling at them. Avoid allowing your demeanor to suggest anger when you are simply experiencing high levels of excitement or frustration.

The manner in which you articulate yourself will establish the atmosphere in which the conversation unfolds. Should your demeanor exhibit frustration and anger, your partner will instinctively adopt a defensive stance. This does not facilitate effective communication. Preserve a sense of openness and sincerity, demonstrate appropriate emotional expression to enhance the effectiveness of your communication, while maintaining a consistent and confident demeanor.

The higher the level of assurance you possess in relation to the subject matter being discussed with your partner, the greater the probability that you will sustain a balanced demeanor. Consider all potential reactions from your partner and strategize how you will effectively address each of them. The greater your confidence in your preparation, the more effectively you will sustain a composed demeanor and effectively articulate your message.

Body Language

When engaging in a discourse with your marital partner regarding a significant matter, it is imperative to ensure that you maintain receptivity to their viewpoint and reaction. Assuming an open posture with arms either extended to the sides or resting in a relaxed manner on your lap will contribute to their comfort and indicate your receptiveness to their response. Your partner is likely to possess exceptional knowledge about you and exhibit superior proficiency in interpreting your nonverbal cues compared to most individuals.

Active Listening

Active listening is arguably the most crucial component of efficient communication in your interpersonal relationships. Numerous individuals engage in listening with the intention of providing a response, whereas the suitable approach to attaining effective communication involves listening with the objective of comprehending. Attentively consider the responses provided by your spouse and then recapitulate the information for their benefit.

For instance, "I comprehend that you harbor doubts regarding this proposal." When individuals experience uncertainty, they will confirm it and presumably elaborate on the underlying reasons. If they do not have any uncertainty, they will proceed to rectify and elucidate their thoughts in an alternative manner. Exhibiting attentive listening in this manner holds significant importance towards fostering effective communication within your interpersonal connections.

Example Conversation

Take into account this illustrative dialogue pertaining to a prospective relocation being discussed between a married couple. This exemplar dialogue skillfully demonstrates the utilization of the four key components of proficient communication.

Husband: I would appreciate the opportunity to converse with you about a matter that my supervisor brought up earlier today. Please take note of the term "discuss." This choice is more appropriate than using the word "talk" as it effectively conveys an open dialogue rather than a one-sided dissemination of information.

Husband: I am being evaluated for a potential advancement in my professional position. However, it would entail relocating to a different municipality. If I choose to accept it, it will occur within the following two months.

Spouse: It is my sincere preference to avoid relocating our children amidst the ongoing academic term. Could it wait?

Husband: While I acknowledge your reluctance to relocate the children at present, there is a concern that they may not be able to defer their relocation indefinitely. Please take note of the utilization of active listening.

Husband: Apart from the aforementioned, do you have any reservations? What are your thoughts? He assumes a posture in which his arms are modestly extended and his hands remain deliberately distanced. The individual's nonverbal cues are encouraging her to express her viewpoints.

Spouse: It would be greatly appreciated if you could enhance your professional trajectory and attain greater financial security. Perhaps we could possibly reach an agreement regarding the educational aspect.

During the course of this dialogue, the husband shall endeavor to maintain a congenial and hospitable vocal demeanor. This does not constitute a dictatorship, but rather signifies an inclusive deliberation regarding a potential relocation. It is imperative to communicate this by means of appropriate tone and body language to avert conflicts.

Parents

Engaging in dialogues with parents can pose challenges, even in adulthood. You aim to effectively communicate your thoughts and solicit their guidance and input, while concurrently asserting your maturity and distinction as an adult. Simultaneously, it is imperative to manifest the same level of esteem and regard that was ingrained during your formative years. Maintaining a subtle equilibrium, proficient communication skills can significantly facilitate your progress.

Word Choice

The primary factor to be mindful of when selecting words while conversing with one's parents pertains to the utilization of colloquial expressions. The evolution of vernacular language varies across generations. If one employs colloquial language and idiomatic expressions specific to their generation while communicating with their parents, it is probable that the intended message would not be comprehended by them.

Rather than employing colloquial language, consider seeking alternative expressions to convey your thoughts. If engaged in a conversation with your parents and you happen to express something using colloquial language, promptly consider an alternative manner of articulating it that adheres to a more standard form of English. It becomes increasingly manageable through consistent practice.

One effective method to assist in selecting appropriate vocabulary within such circumstances is to engage in the practice of journaling and engaging in brainstorming exercises. Consider colloquial expressions and idiomatic phrases that are typically employed in informal conversations with friends and romantic partners and outline an extensive compilation of alternative expressions devoid of informal language. Engaging in this practice periodically over the course of several weeks will cultivate the appropriate frame of mind required to effectively eliminate colloquial language from your discourse as and when required.

Tone

Regardless of one's deep-seated enthusiasm, it is crucial to maintain a composed demeanor when engaging in conversation with one's parents. Parents will certainly be displeased by a tone of voice that is excessively enthusiastic or agitated. Although you may have reached adulthood, it is customary for them to expect a specific degree of deference from you. Your vocal inflection effectively conveys a sense of respect towards them.

It is recommended to refrain from exhibiting elevated vocal expressions when discussing subjects that evoke enthusiasm. Maintain an equitable and deliberate pace of speech to ensure comprehensibility. Ensure that you are bestowing upon them the full measure of respect that they anticipate and merit.

Body Language

It is highly probable that, as a grown individual, when engaging in discussions of significance with one's parents, the underlying intention is to solicit their guidance. Maintain an inclusive and receptive demeanor to convey your willingness to accept their response in any manner they choose. Maintain a posture where your hands are either clasped in your lap or placed gracefully at your sides. If you encounter difficulty in maintaining your hands by your sides, consider interlocking them behind your back or in front of your persona.

Active Listening

This attribute of effective communication is likely to be most effortless when engaging in dialogue with your parents. Having been an attentive listener to them throughout your entire life, it should be effortless to ensure that you are presently engaged in active listening. Please reiterate the advice provided by them to ensure comprehension of their message.

Example Conversation

In this exemplar dialogue, a young lady is seeking counsel from her parents regarding the prospect of a potential alteration in her academic major at the university. Observe the utilization of the four characteristics of proficient communication throughout the discourse.

Daughter: I would greatly appreciate some guidance. There has been an emergence of an opportunity at educational institution, and I am uncertain whether I should seize it. In her statement, she precisely articulates the intended objective of the discussion, demonstrating a careful selection of vocabulary.

Mother: May I inquire about the nature of this chance?

Daughter: A professor has recommended that I possess exceptional aptitude in the field of chemical engineering. I derived great satisfaction from attending his class, and I achieved notable success in it. He is of the opinion that I should alter my academic trajectory and pursue a profession in bioengineering rather than nursing. What do you think? The daughter extends her hands with an air of curiousity, beckoning for replies.

Father: Are you sufficiently satisfied with it to make a complete shift in your professional trajectory? It has always been your aspiration to pursue a career in nursing.

Daughter: I comprehend that you have reservations about the impulsive nature of my decision. After careful consideration, I remain committed to serving others. Engaging in attentive listening and conveying an understanding of their concerns.

Father: Could you please elaborate on the disparity in remuneration and educational qualifications? Can you indicate whether you would prefer to allocate additional or decreased time to your educational pursuits? What potential for career progression exists within the organization?

Daughter: I have not yet devoted significant consideration to the matter. I'm really not sure.

Mother: I advise you to conduct further research prior to finalizing your decision. We are fully prepared to provide our support for any decision you make, however, it is crucial to approach this significant matter with due deliberation and caution.

Daughter: I appreciate your efforts in helping me see things from a different angle. I will make an effort to obtain some answers. Talk soon? Respectful and inquisitive tone.

Observe the daughter's effective utilization of succinct and lucid sentences in order to communicate her message to her parents. She refrained from employing colloquial language and maintained a precise, composed, and inquisitive demeanor throughout the dialogue.

Are you considering engaging the services of a public relations agency?
As previously observed, there are two alternatives available in regard to managing your PR strategy and execution – the first option being to internally manage the process with the aid of a team of skilled PR and corporate communication professionals, while the second option involves engaging the services of an external agency to completely outsource the task.
We will examine the factors and criteria you should or should not take into account if you opt to manage your communications with the assistance of a Public Relations agency.
Is your PR advisor asserting that regardless of the circumstances, they will ensure comprehensive media

coverage for your company, essentially guaranteeing a specified amount of newspaper column space?

Nothing could be further from an overt falsehood, and truthfully, public relations never operates in such a manner in formal settings.

any region across the world. Indeed, if you possess a comprehensive and enduring public relations/communication strategy for your organization, it is imperative to steadfastly refrain from engaging with entities that promise guaranteed "column space coverage."

Consider the media (along with the community of journalists) to be the ultimate recipients of your content. They are subject to their own limitations in terms of creative expression. This ultimately becomes a dynamic involving sophisticated content, indispensable advertisers (who secure a substantial portion of the advertising space), and the editor, who possesses the authority to determine what the reader ought to be exposed to and informed about.

A similar comparison can be made across various forms of media encompassing print, television, and online platforms, among others. Moreover, compounded by the ceaseless growth, we must also contend with the mounting weight of competition within our respective sector.

Amidst all of this, should an individual approach you and provide an assurance of unquestionable coverage, it would only be plausible if one were naive enough to believe that any of us within the public relations industry possess such influential powers.

It is an undeniable reality that none of us possess that attribute, and to a certain degree, it would be disrespectful to the media's capacity for autonomous thought to entertain such a notion.

We have the potential to serve as consultants for your company's public image, yet primarily function as intermediaries to media contacts—occasionally disseminating information that we deem valuable, and occasionally extending assistance when requested.

We exclusively serve the content requirements of the journalist community, catering to their specified preferences.

Throughout this process, we have also demonstrated adeptness in strategically addressing our client's public relations requirements and providing an experienced approach in generating media-focused content that is both pertinent and consumable.

View public relations advisors as collaborative partners in the successful implementation of your comprehensive long-term communication strategy. I do not possess the ability to effortlessly generate immediate media coverage at my disposal. I would like to clarify that no public relations advisor possesses such a mythical power.

Public relations agencies of various types and sizes may continue to express interest in collaborating with your organization, with the intention of participating in your communication strategy and implementation. We have consistently observed that organizations actively seek these attributes: does your agency possess the necessary magnitude, scope, and global reach to effectively engage across all media platforms, including social media, in every geographical region worldwide?

It is imperative to verify the credentials of your potential agency, as it is crucial to ensure that nothing is amiss. Furthermore, it is essential to take into consideration that the agency must possess the capability and flexibility to effectively handle public relations strategy and implementation for an organization of your nature.

Although you have the opportunity to engage the most exceptional agency in existence, it is crucial to consider whether their expertise aligns harmoniously with the size and capabilities of your company. Furthermore, it is worth considering whether their capabilities are tailored more towards larger corporations rather than the unique service offerings or distinguishing qualities of your niche, small organization.

Thus, it is advisable to assess the following criteria when considering engaging the services of a PR agency.

Has the agency demonstrated a track record of delivering substantive public relations value to companies similar to yours, and with what frequency have they achieved this?

Do they possess the requisite nimbleness - not merely in their playing style, but do they appear to align with your strategic vision - would they discover harmonious collaboration while working alongside a client such as yourself?

Do they possess a level of dedication to effectively collaborate with companies such as yours over an extended duration, thereby enabling you to ultimately reap the true advantages of partnering with an agency? Alternatively, if your objective is solely to obtain sporadic instances of media coverage, the necessity of dedicating time towards evaluating the agency could be eliminated.

Do they possess the requisite skills to unlearn and adapt according to your requirements? This is so important. Whether one approves of it or not, significant and worldwide agencies possess a particular perspective, and despite their willingness to exert effort, they may not be inclined to cater to your unique communication requirements.

Do they possess a comprehensive comprehension of the specific requirements of your industry, and are they amenable to dedicating the necessary time and effort to acquire a profound understanding of your media visibility prerequisites?

Is their primary focus solely on delivering standard and generic releases? Do they acquire comprehensive knowledge about your profile, discern the most effective strategies for you, and present you in the most favorable light?

To what extent can they contribute additional credibility and augment the value of their image, not only in the short term but over a span of 2-3 years?

Are they contemporary? Do they actively engage in supporting the news industry's crowd-sourcing initiatives?

If your requirements are specific to the local area, do they possess knowledge regarding successful strategies in that particular market or geography?

Occasionally, a seemingly straightforward endeavor in a specific geographical region may prove unattainable in alternate locations. And it is imperative that they display a willingness to communicate this directly and honestly to you.

Do they discuss practical and feasible approaches to communication work? Occasionally, major agencies excel at orchestrating large-scale events, resulting in a sudden surge of visibility; however, the benefits obtained from such endeavors are negligible.

Therefore, if you are considering engaging a PR agency to assist with your strategic communication endeavors, carefully reflect upon these inquiries and ensure that you possess a comprehensive comprehension of the anticipated worth and intricacies involved.

The Origin of its Source

People adopt a propensity to prioritize the satisfaction of others for a variety of reasons. There does not exist a single underlying factor responsible for these inclinations. They typically stem from a combination of various factors, which include the subsequent:

Past Experiences of Trauma

People-pleasing tendencies can occasionally emerge as a result of a fear-induced reaction linked to certain traumatic experiences. If an individual has ever undergone trauma such as child abuse or domestic violence, they may experience difficulty in establishing a sense of safety when it comes to establishing personal boundaries. One may have discerned that adhering to the desires of others and disregarding one's own needs was a more prudent choice. It is probable that you have discovered that maintaining a constant effort to accommodate others has resulted in feelings of security and popularity.

Problems with Self-Esteem

Occasionally, individuals exhibit tendencies towards people-pleasing due to a lack of appreciation for their own aspirations and requirements. As a result of an absence of self-assurance, individuals who frequently seek to please others require external validation, and they may hold the belief that engaging in actions for the sake of others will pave the way for recognition and inclusion.

Apprehension of potential rejection

An individual may adopt a tendency towards pleasing others if they possess a deep-rooted apprehension of facing rejection. This apprehension stems from a fundamental absence of self-assurance. They make efforts to accommodate others due to concerns that their failure to surpass expectations may result in unfavorable opinions.

Indication of a Psychiatric Disorder

This conduct may indicate the presence of a mental health disorder such as anxiety, depression, avoidant personality disorder, borderline personality disorder (BPD), or dependent personality disorder.

Methods for Ceasing

If you desire to alter the cycle of prioritizing the satisfaction of others at the detriment of your own well-being, it is imperative that you develop the ability to discern and recognize these behaviors as they manifest. By enhancing your understanding of your tendency to seek approval, you can initiate modifications. "Listed below are several methods to accomplish this objective:

Demonstrate genuine compassion if your intentions are sincere.

It is acceptable to cultivate acts of benevolence. It is essential to comprehend that kindness does not originate from a desire to obtain someone's validation. Typically, it does not encompass any additional intention aside from aiming to enhance someone's quality of life.

Prior to extending your assistance, it is advisable to reflect upon your motives and the corresponding emotions they elicit within you. Will this opportunity to provide aid result in a sense of joy for you? Would you experience any resentment if the individual you are providing assistance to does not reciprocate?

Put Yourself First

If you aspire to assist others, it is imperative that you possess emotional reserves and vitality. Failure to prioritize self-care will hinder your ability to attend to the needs of others. Prioritizing oneself is not an act of selfishness, but rather a means of self-care in order to effectively assist others.

It is permissible to exhibit compassion and generosity towards others, nevertheless, it is equally imperative to attend to and respect one's own needs. These requirements may encompass offering your viewpoint during a meeting, cultivating self-assurance in expressing your sentiments and emotions, and articulating your needs within a interpersonal context.

Set Boundaries

Establishing robust boundaries is imperative for conquering one's inclination towards excessive people-pleasing. When an individual solicits your assistance, or when you find yourself tempted to intercede in a given situation, take a moment to contemplate:

Your perspective on the matter. Do you sincerely desire to pursue this course of action, or does the mere contemplation of it induce a sense of apprehension within you?

Would you be able to allocate sufficient time for self-care? Will you be required to allocate precious time or refrain from completing an essential task?
What are the emotional effects of aiding others? Do you experience feelings of resentment or joy?

Stop Volunteering

Irrespective of the nature of the issue, you consistently exhibit preparedness to offer solutions to others. You consistently offer your services for professional responsibilities, or you provide recommendations whenever a friend or acquaintance discloses a challenge.

On future instances, endeavor to test your limits and refrain from proactively providing assistance until solicited by others. When your partner begins expressing dissatisfaction with their employer, demonstrate empathy by actively listening rather than offering advice on how to address the issue. It is highly probable that their primary intention is to seek validation or empathy above all else.

Find A Therapist

Breaking patterns that have been established for an extended period of time is a task of considerable difficulty, particularly so when it involves overcoming patterns formed during childhood or as a result of traumatic experiences. Engaging in a therapeutic conversation has the potential to facilitate the exploration and understanding of your propensity to consistently prioritize the happiness of others. Despite the absence of a discernible cause, they possess the ability to provide valuable counsel or strategies to assist you in recognizing the precise behaviors you employ in order to seek the approval of others.

Engaging in self-sacrifice with the sole purpose of pleasing others is not advantageous for anyone involved. If you frequently experience persistent feelings of frustration and dissatisfaction due to the incessant need to ensure the satisfaction of others, it would be prudent to engage in a conversation with a mental health professional regarding efficacious strategies to address and resolve your people-pleasing tendencies, ultimately leading to the attainment of genuine happiness.

6. PLEASANT GESTURES DISPLAYED BY WOMEN

What is typically considered as displaying \\"amicable\\" nonverbal communication by individuals? "Presented below are a selection of practices that are enticing and congenial in various social, professional, and personal situations:

Grinning

Displaying a wide range of facial expressions

Maintaining a position where your hands are positioned below the level of your jawline (as having them above might be perceived as excessive or assertive).

Minor arm folding

It is important to refrain from placing one's hands inside pockets.

Triple nodding to indicate engagement.

Observe attentively, directing one's gaze from the eyes to the mouth and then to the body.

Demonstrating a propensity for the other person

Unobtrusive reflecting

I was once enlightened by a wise woman who made it known to me that an individual's nonverbal cues can be exceedingly revealing in virtually all circumstances, particularly during romantic encounters. The astute individual: Patti Wood, a highly skilled expert in interpreting body language and the esteemed author of Success Signals: A Guide to Reading Body Language. (In light of her book title, it can be reasonably inferred that she possesses knowledge on the subject, although this is merely a speculative notion.)

As an unmarried individual who frequently engages in dating, I wholeheartedly concur that in almost all circumstances, a gentleman's nonverbal cues on Tinder provide me with a comprehensive understanding of his character and intentions. (Aside from his profile, which serves as evidence of his fondness for The Office.) How unique).

This presumably pertains to the manner in which body language mirrors the sentinel of an individual's internal reflections, even when no explicit communication is intentionally conveyed. It is the kind of situation where individuals express their emotions through non-verbal cues such as gestures, smiles, nods, and similar actions, rather than explicitly stating it. Furthermore, I don't know about all of you, but I would greatly prefer to engage in a romantic relationship with someone who consistently demonstrates their caring nature, rather than merely verbalizing it.

If you, too, wish to engage in the realm of nonverbal communication, it is crucial to be alert to various indicators and patterns. Below, discover the areas to which specialists strongly advise paying close attention in order to ascertain whether the individual with whom you feel a connection genuinely reciprocates your sentiments.

1. His stance is open.

The implication is that one should maintain a stance where the feet are positioned at a width equivalent to the shoulders, the shoulders should be relaxed, the hands and arms must not be crossed, and the jaw should be unclenched. According to an accredited expert, Shamyra Howard, the founder of Use Your Mouth, individuals who display open body language demonstrate genuine interest and attentiveness towards you.

2. You can truly witness the movements of his hands.

Consider it a notion deserving of gratitude that, during your time spent with this individual, they refrain from idling with their hands tucked away in their pockets or acting in contradiction to their sincere intentions. Howard asserts that when someone is amicable in your presence, their hands tend to be conspicuous. Therefore, acquire those small objects promptly and place them on the table within your line of sight.

3. He angles his head in two manners.

Are you aware that canines exhibit a charming head tilt when they encounter a novel sound? Rest assured, as companions in this context can be likened to our affectionate canines. When an individual inclines their head laterally, it demonstrates their inclination and attentiveness. It is evident that you are actively engaging their analytical hemisphere of the brain, thus it would be advisable to cooperate with this predisposition.

4. His breathing is loose.

When his respiration exhibits a moderate rhythm, it signifies that he is relaxed and able to conduct himself authentically in your presence. According to relationship expert and psychotherapist Melissa Divaris Thompson, "This is a positive indication, as men derive pleasure from experiencing positive emotions when they are in the company of their partners."

5. He has damp hands.

If his palms are moist when you are strolling along the street, it may indicate that he is physically warm, but it could also indicate that he is anxious. According to Thompson, "Exhibiting apprehension can be interpreted as a sign of genuine interest and a lack of intention to cause any harm."

6. He fortuitously intersects or makes contact with you.

Irrespective of whether he unintentionally makes contact with your hand or cannot refrain from tapping your foot beneath the table, it is a significant indication of physical closeness as it demonstrates his genuine desire to be near you, according to Thompson.

7. He engages in the act of adjusting his tie.

According to David Bennett, a consultant and relationship expert, individuals tend to engage in self-soothing by placing their hands on the area where the neck and collarbones meet, when they feel anxious. Due to the positioning of the bowtie, individuals may frequently adjust their ties when deeply infatuated with a lady and perturbed by this predicament.

8. He exhibits an unsteady flow of words. If he consistently exhibits significant difficulty in articulating his words despite typically being the center of attention, it suggests that he experiences anxiety in your presence. According to Bennett, if you come to the realization that he is not behaving in a typically abnormal manner but instead seems disoriented and struggles to articulate his thoughts in your presence, this could be regarded as a sign of interest.

9. His countenance becomes flushed... and not due to the ambient temperature. According to Bennett, an intense attraction towards someone may trigger a physiological reaction resulting in increased pressure and the release of adrenaline, ultimately leading to a

flushed complexion. However, prior to drawing any hasty conclusions, it is imperative to verify that the angle is not precisely 90 degrees and that he has not consumed his third serving of tequila.

10. He retreats from you when you are face to face.

Whether waiting in queue at a dining establishment, riding on public transportation, bidding farewell, or in any given scenario, he is unable to resist the temptation to be in close proximity to your visage within reasonable bounds. According to online dating coach Andi Forness, if he does not have a fear of physical intimacy and openly communicates his desires, even if they are not extreme, it is logical that he would want to take advantage of being as near to you as one would reasonably expect in the given situation.

11. His understudies are tremendous.

It is conceivable that you may find yourself in a challenging situation, or that this subtle indication suggests his romantic interest in you. "Enlargement is a neural response that occurs when an individual experiences a liking and attraction towards something," explains Wood.

12. He displays a noticeable elevation of his eyebrows upon catching sight of you.

If he harbors a preference for you and admires the aspects he observes in your presence, it implies he desires a more substantial presence of your being. "Subsequently, a gradual revelation occurred, prompting the elevation of his eyebrows," Wood remarks. This also suggests that he is interested in whatever you are saying.

13. He assumes a defensive stance whenever he smiles.

According to Wood, individuals tend to stop smiling in this manner around the age of 5, unless they are genuinely happy. It is unlikely that he would exhibit a vibrant smile while casually engaging in playful banter, although this may occur during an exceptionally enchanting outing when he is thoroughly enjoying himself. "When he experiences genuine joy, he does not hide it," Wood stated, emphasizing the need to search for telltale signs of happiness.

14. He smiles broadly.

Authentic smiles extend beyond the lips, elevating the temples and causing a slight crinkling of the eyes. If his smile encompasses his entire countenance, it signifies that you are exerting a significant positive influence on him.

15. He gently moistens his lips in an endearing manner.

According to Wood, when one develops a strong attraction towards someone, there is an increase in salivary secretion. In accordance with this, he might promptly apply his tongue to his lips or firmly bring them together.

16. He gazes upon your visage, focusing not on your eyes, but on your countenance.

You may perceive that an individual who is profoundly captivated by you may find it challenging to divert his gaze. Nevertheless, as a result of people's inclination towards constant engagement with their mobile devices, maintaining unwavering eye contact can elicit discomfort in individuals. In accordance with the aforementioned, a recent directive states that if approximately 80% of an individual's attention during your interaction is directed towards transitioning between your eyes, nose, and lips, it can be inferred that they possess a romantic interest in you, as clarified by Wood.

17. He inhales deeply upon encountering your presence.

Indeed, it is undeniable that men necessitate oxygen. Nevertheless, when he unconsciously inhales deeply, he will contract his stomach and expand his chest. This subconscious technique aims to create the illusion of a broader chest and a narrower waist, two attributes that enhance his physical fitness and, from a perspective of human development, increase his perceived attractiveness, according to Wood's analysis. Overall, he has a genuine interest in you and is making an effort to capture your attention.

18. Once he catches sight of you, he must promptly get in touch with you or simply observe you attentively.

According to Wood, individuals' actions upon entering a place reflect their values and priorities. He will not casually enter your premises and establish himself without first engaging in an embrace, kiss, or prolonged gaze.

19. He demonstrates a tendency to lean in your direction while engaged in conversation.

In a noisy establishment such as a bar, this sign is unlikely to carry much significance. Nevertheless, when he is able to hear you clearly and attentively leans in, it indicates that he is genuinely interested in what you have to say, as well as in you as a whole.

20. Place your hands upon your hips, ensuring that your elbows extend outward to the sides.

According to Wood, assuming this position, where one's arms are not pressed against their sides, suggests a greater physical presence, thus indicating a male force signal. They employ it to demonstrate tangible superiority over various individuals of the male gender. In this particular situation, and assuming he is deliberate in his actions towards you, it signifies that he is seeking your attention.

21. He makes physical contact with your knee or gently tucks a strand of your hair behind your ear.

According to Wood, when he initiates physical contact under the guise of providing a different explanation (for instance, to praise the delicate nature of your jeans), it is an attempt to gauge your response to his touch. According to Wood, contact serves as a tool for evaluating your personal boundaries, suggesting that he may simply have a strong interest in engaging in sexual activity. Nevertheless, if he harbors genuine affection for you, he may exhibit a more gradual withdrawal and present a polite smile while doing so, indicating his intention to invest time and effort in establishing a closer connection with you.

22. He assumes a seated posture with his legs extended apart.
This exposed his genitalia, which contain numerous delicate and sensitive regions. The position he holds is one of vulnerability that suggests he will make genuine efforts to familiarize himself with you, both outwardly and internally. (Alternatively, it's possible that he is engaging in an expression of male privilege by unnecessarily occupying extra space with his posture.)

23. He directs his pelvic region towards you.
Due to its inherently sexual nature, this body part frequently indicates sexual attraction or a lack thereof, as stated by Wood. If he disengages his hips from you, it is highly probable that the latter option is correct.

24. He carefully directs his toes towards you.
The lower extremities become involved in the fight-or-flight response that is triggered when one is placed in a dangerous situation, thus they are mainly influenced by the subconscious

mind—and can provide significant insights into social interactions. "According to Wood, it is typically observed that the feet tend to align with the intended direction of the heart." Evidently, the timing holds great importance in this situation. When engaging in conversation with an individual who initially displays interest, if you proceed to make physical contact with their arm and subsequently observe their feet pointing away from you, it can be inferred from the context that their interest has diminished.

25. He folds his legs.

If he positions himself in a manner that angles his torso and middle section away from you, there is a possibility that he is not engaged or involved. However, in the event that he retracts his legs and redirects the remaining part of his body towards you, it may suggest that he is simply exhibiting signs of shyness. However, this is contingent upon the individual.

26. He adjusts his position towards you while you are engaged in conversation.

It is evident that he should undoubtedly approach you in closer proximity.

27. He engages in dialogue with you without directly challenging you.

Although it might indicate that he is considering other options, Wood advises against hastily forming opinions about someone who engages in captivating conversation while also showing interest in others. If he demonstrates active engagement in seeking out prevailing concepts or poses numerous inquiries, his nonverbal cues may reflect his innate humility and genuine interest in you.

28. He contacts his throat.

Wood asserts that the throat serves as a means of communication and vulnerability. Should he happen to encounter it during your collaboration, he is greatly interested in you and anxious about making a positive impression. In any event, once again, the setting can play a vital role: If you are speaking with a participant, a throat gesture could indicate disdain. Thus, acquire knowledge about his condition and observe various indications within this comprehensive analysis prior to offering him consolation.

29. Upon his touch, his palm firmly presses against yours, intertwining your fingers.

This particular handshake conveys an inclination to establish a connection. The aforementioned statement also applies to fingers that are interlocked. Conversely, a palm oriented at an angle conveys indications of fear or potential concealment.

30. During the course of his conversation, he inadvertently makes contact with your lower arm with his hand.

The message is explicitly and unmistakably conveyed: He seeks your attention, whether to captivate you or to ensure your attentive listening—because he desires to be heard.

31. He leisurely walks alongside you.

According to Wood, if he consistently maintains a lead of two strides ahead of you, it suggests that his primary concern is his own well-being rather than yours. If he is not navigating you through a hazardous or congested area, he should adjust his motion to align with yours.

32. He consistently positions himself beside you whenever feasible.

Irrespective of the presence of a cozy sofa adjacent to your petite loveseat, he consistently opts to snuggle up in close proximity to you. In the event that you find yourself in a coffee shop equipped with booths, he will opt for sitting adjacently rather than opposite to your position. This is indicative of him belonging to the same 'group' as you, Wood asserts.

33. He engages in manipulation of his glass.

Wood suggests that this phenomenon may serve as an indication of heightened anxiousness or engrossment. It is advisable that he get in touch with you in the event of a stroke.

34. His vocal timbre transitions to a more deliberate and refined resonance.

Wood highlights that through this act of generosity, he demonstrates his ability to relinquish his role as a guardian and embrace vulnerability in your relationship.

35. He actively curtails disruptions and disturbances.

In addition to neglecting his phone etiquette in your presence, a glaring lack of basic courtesy, he also refuses to lend attention to your account while commenting on the football game unfolding behind you or the excessive heat of the Cajun fries. Despite this, regardless of whether he encroaches upon your personal space (as we are all fallible beings), a genuinely interested gentleman will promptly offer his apologies and initiate contact with you, demonstrating his sincere desire to re-establish a connection, as stated by Wood.

36. He respects your assets and treats them with deferential regard.

Irrespective of whether he goes out of his way to make you feel like royalty on a first date, pay attention to his treatment of your belongings. Instead of handing you the coat, does he throw it to you? Does he illicitly confiscate gum from your handbag and subsequently discard it on the ground? Wood asserts that the negligent treatment of your possessions reveals the level of esteem he possesses for you. Furthermore, it provides insight into the hypothetical scenario of cohabitation.

Treasure Hunt

A leader or captain is selected to assume responsibility for providing direction. He/she ought to arrange the group in pairs, with the aim of facilitating collaborative efforts and fostering a sense of mutual understanding to attain the desired outcome. The members of the group will be kindly requested to vacate the designated gaming area for a duration of five minutes, after which they may regroup.

The leader/captain shall carefully retrieve the compact and lightweight items present in the vicinity, concealing them discreetly at strategic locations. Subsequently, the leader/captain shall signal the group, granting permission for their re-entry.

They are required to collaborate in pairs in order to locate all of the concealed items. This will enable the child or adolescent with Asperger's syndrome to comprehend the possibility of building mutual trust and establishing personal relationships based on shared interests, which ultimately facilitates the attainment of the intended objective.

They will have the capacity to perceive their partner as a collaborator, with whom they can engage in empathetic collaboration, provided they possess the requisite resources.

The conclusion should encompass a brief summary expounding upon the significance and advantages associated with one's ability to place trust in others and foster deep connections based on friendship.

10

DEBATES

Requisite materials required for this dynamic include supporting materials pertaining to the subject matter under consideration.

Minimum number of people:20 and 25 people.

Duration: Approximately 45 minutes.

In order to foster the advancement of this dynamic, the team is bifurcated into two segments, with the appointment of a captain to oversee and facilitate the efficient progress of each group.

We proceed with the selection of a pertinent subject matter that is both contemporary and appealing to a wide audience, encompassing individuals with Asperger's syndrome - as their inclination to engage in conversation is often driven by their specific areas of interest.

The two groups are provided with an explanation that victory will be achieved through collaborative efforts, and it is emphasized that in case any team member encounters uncertainties regarding the answers, their companions are available to provide assistance and assistance to them.

Subsequently, the individuals should proceed to formulate a set of inquiries pertaining to the chosen subject matter that they will pose to the opposing group. These questions must be of mutual interest to both parties as well as provide explicit solutions to each query.

Upon completion of the necessary arrangements, the commencement of the deliberation shall ensue. All participants are required to inquire and respond accordingly; the team that accrues the highest number of accurate responses shall be declared the victor.

The aim is for individuals diagnosed with Asperger's syndrome, specifically children and adolescents, to develop a strong sense of trust and willingness to openly communicate and engage with other members in the group. This will foster the desire to interact, pose questions, make suggestions, actively listen, and occasionally provide feedback in response to the group's recommendations.

This will instill a sense of assurance and motivate individuals to actively engage and collaboratively participate, recognizing the indispensable role of building trustworthy, harmonious, empathetic, and respectful connections with others in our day-to-day existence.

• It is not a grave issue. • This does not present a significant concern. • This is not a matter of great importance.

Given the information presented thus far, it is evident that the contrary holds true. The gravity of OCD is undeniably apparent when considering phrases such as suicide, depression, and job loss. The World Health Organization (WHO) has assigned OCD a position of considerable concern in their rankings of debilitating conditions. Therefore, it is evident that OCD, in all its forms, demands serious attention and must not be trivialized. It is customary for individuals to experience a sense of respite upon receiving a diagnosis of Obsessive-Compulsive Disorder. Their acquaintances may go as far as lightly poking them and making a few lighthearted remarks regarding the condition. This phenomenon can be considered typical, as our perception of OCD may have been influenced by movies and reality TV, leading us to downplay the severity of this condition. A renowned figure in the realm of reality television, Khloe has adopted the new moniker of Khlo C-D. The aforementioned aspects serve to dilute a grave matter that has the potential to result in loss of life. It is prudent to bear in mind that the gravity of OCD should never be disregarded. It is permissible to make lighthearted remarks (with the approval of the individual affected by the disorder) in order to alleviate tension. However, it is essential to provide support to those coping with obsessive-compulsive disorder when circumstances warrant it.

• No Treatment

Those individuals who hold the viewpoint that OCD is an innate personality attribute also maintain that it is thus incumbent upon us to seek out effective means of managing and alleviating OCD symptoms. This is not accurate. While a complete cure for OCD is currently unavailable, there are therapeutic interventions that effectively regulate the disorder, granting individuals afflicted with it a level of relief and the ability to exercise some measure of control over their symptoms. These approaches will be elaborated upon in the forthcoming sections, however, it can be confidently affirmed that extensive clinical research substantiates their efficacy in managing obsessive-compulsive disorder.

• Engaging in activities such as shopping can be indicative of Obsessive-Compulsive Disorder (OCD)

In order for excessive indulgence in shopping to be classified as an obsessive tendency, it would necessitate the absence of pleasure as a prerequisite condition. It would necessitate initiating a contemplation that persists, recurs, and remains persistent, despite the individual's utmost efforts to eliminate these thoughts, yielding no favorable outcomes. Shopping should be utilized only as a final recourse to alleviate the mounting anxiety that ensues when all other avenues have been exhausted. Having a desire to finish a series or engage in unlawful acts, such as taking someone's life, may not necessarily be associated with Obsessive-Compulsive Disorder (OCD). Initially, it is imperative that the thought be intrusive in nature, progressing subsequently to an obsessive state, while inducing significant anxiety within the individual, who possesses an awareness of the illogicality or even illicitness of said obsessions. Subsequently, it is necessary for the aforementioned condition to trigger an irresistible compulsion, whether in the form of action or thought, in order to mitigate the anxiety. Furthermore, the frequency at which this compulsion occurs must reach a level where it significantly hampers the individual's ability to lead a satisfactory quality of life.

www.ingramcontent.com/pod-product-compliance
Lightning Source LLC
Chambersburg PA
CBHW050234120526
44590CB00016B/2089